Voices for Freedom

Abolitionist Heroes

By Geoffrey
M. Horn

Sojourner Truth

Speaking Up for Freedom

CRABTREE
Publishing Company
www.crabtreebooks.com

Author: Geoffrey Michael Horn
Publishing plan research and development:
    Sean Charlebois, Reagan Miller
    Crabtree Publishing Company
Editors: Mark Sachner, Lynn Peppas
Proofreader: Ellen Rodger
Editorial director: Kathy Middleton
Photo research: Ruth Owen
Designer: Westgrapix/Tammy West
Production coordinator: Margaret Amy Salter
Production: Kim Richardson
Curriculum adviser: Suzy Gazlay, M.A.
Editorial consultant: James Marten, Ph.D.; Chair, Department
    of History, Marquette University, Milwaukee, Wisconsin

Front cover (inset), back cover, and title page: Photograph of
Sojourner Truth.
Front cover (bottom): A series of anti-slavery trading cards from
the 1800s, by American artist Henry Louis Stephens. Pictures like
this were used by abolitionists to convince people that slavery
should be stopped.

Written, developed, and produced by Water Buffalo Books

Photographs and reproductions
Alamy: page 19; page 29 (bottom); page 31; page 39. The Architect
of the Capitol: page 44 (bottom). Corbis: page 5; page 14; page 18;
page 45; page 56 (top). Courtesy of the Library of Congress: Image
3c19343: page 3; page 4 (top left); Image 3c19343: page 6; Image
3a20849: page 8; Image 08979: page 9; Image 08978: page 10; Image
01264: page 11 (bottom); Image 3c19343: page 12 (top left); Image
3a06254: page 15 (left); Image 160052: page 15 (right); Image
3g02525: page 16 (bottom); Image 3c19343: page 20 (top left);
Image 3a18408: page 22 (top); Image 00057: page 24 (top); Image
3g02524: page 25; poster: page 26 (bottom); appeal: page 27 (top);
Image 3b42488: page 27 (center); Image 01038: page 28 (top); Image
3c19343: page 29 (top left); Image 00267: page 32 (top); Image
3a13519: page 32 (bottom); Image 3c20350: page 35; Image 3c19343:
page 39 (top left); Image 3a12743: page 40 (top); Image 3a10460:
page 46; Image 3a18122: page 47; Image 3a13608: page 48; Image
3c19343: page 50 (top left); Image 3a29554: page 50 (bottom);
Infantry: page 53 (top); Image 3a18453: page 54; Image 3b10666:
page 55. Getty Images: page 13; page 20; page 37; page 43 (top).
The Granger Collection: page 52 (bottom). Bryan Haeffele (Hudson
Valley.org): page 17. Historic Northampton: page 40 (bottom).
NASA: page 57. North Wind Archives: page 12 (bottom); page 22
(bottom); page 23; page 24 (bottom); page 26 (top); page 28
(bottom); page 34 (top); page 49 (top). Public domain: page 44
(top). Shutterstock: pages 12-13 (background); page 21; page 38;
page 51. Sojourner Truth Institute: page 11 (top); page 33; page 41;
page 42; page 43 (bottom); page 49 (bottom); page 52 (top); page 53
(bottom); page 56 (bottom). Sojourner Truth Library: page 7; page
16 (top); page 30; page 58. Superstock: page 4. Wikipedia (public
domain): page 34 (bottom); page 36.

Library and Archives Canada Cataloguing in Publication

Horn, Geoffrey M.
    Sojourner Truth : speaking up for freedom / Geoffrey Michael
Horn.

(Voices for freedom: abolitionist heros)
Includes index.
ISBN 978-0-7787-4824-3 (bound).--ISBN 978-0-7787-4840-3 (pbk.)

    1. Truth, Sojourner, d. 1883--Juvenile literature. 2. African
American abolitionists--Biography--Juvenile literature. 3. Aboli-
tionists--United States--Biography--Juvenile literature. 4. African
American women--Biography--Juvenile literature. 5. Social reform-
ers--United States--Biography--Juvenile literature. I. Title. II.
Series: Voices for freedom: abolitionist heros

E185.97.T8H67 2009   j306.3'62092   C2009-903380-1

Library of Congress Cataloging-in-Publication Data

Horn, Geoffrey M.
  Sojourner Truth : speaking up for freedom / Geoffrey Michael Horn.
      p. cm. -- (Voices for freedom. Abolitionist heros)
  Includes index.
  ISBN 978-0-7787-4840-3 (pbk. : alk. paper) -- ISBN 978-0-7787-
4824-3 (reinforced library binding : alk. paper)
  1. Truth, Sojourner, d. 1883--Juvenile literature. 2. African Ameri-
can abolitionists--Biography--Juvenile literature. 3. Abolitionists--
United States--Biography--Juvenile literature. 4. African American
women--Biography--Juvenile literature. 5. Social reformers--
United States--Biography--Juvenile literature. I. Title. II. Series.

E185.97.T8H67 2010
305.5'67092--dc22
[B]
                                                    2009022428

Crabtree Publishing Company
www.crabtreebooks.com   1-800-387-7650

**Published
in Canada**
Crabtree Publishing
616 Welland Ave.
St. Catharines, Ontario
L2M 5V6

**Published in
the United States**
Crabtree Publishing
PMB16A
350 Fifth Ave., Suite 3308
New York, NY 10118

**Published in the
United Kingdom**
Crabtree Publishing
Maritime House
Basin Road North, Hove
BN41 1WR

**Published
in Australia**
Crabtree Publishing
386 Mt. Alexander Rd.
Ascot Vale (Melbourne)
VIC 3032

Contents

J. Albert Adams
Academy Media Center

CHAPTER ONE

A Self-Made Woman

During her lifetime, Sojourner Truth often heard people described as "self-made men." These successful men had not come from rich and powerful families. They had not gone to the finest schools. They had overcome the kinds of obstacles and handicaps that held many other people back.

A Self-Made Woman

Why had they succeeded where so many others failed? In a talk called "Self-Made Men" that he gave in 1859, the abolitionist Frederick Douglass offered a simple answer: "We may explain success mainly by one word and that word is WORK! WORK!! WORK!!! WORK!!!!"

This splendid bronze statue of Sojourner Truth stands in Monument Park in Battle Creek, Michigan. Truth bought a house near Battle Creek in 1857 and lived there for many years.

Most American slaves lived in the South and worked on cotton plantations such as the one shown here. Sojourner Truth's life was different. She lived in the North, and her field work as a slave included growing grains, flax, and tobacco.

Harriet Beecher Stowe—who, like Douglass, was a friend and supporter of Truth—struck a similar theme in a book she published in 1872. The book discussed some of the great men of her time, including Douglass and Abraham Lincoln. She called her book *The Lives and Deeds of Our Self-Made Men.*

Sojourner Truth had her own answer to all this talk about self-made men. Hearing yet another man described as self-made, she said, "Well, I am a self-made woman."

Working for Change

Sojourner Truth was one of the most remarkable women of her era. She was born at the end of the 1700s, when the United States was a new nation. At that time, slavery existed in both the South and the North, including New York state. Truth was a slave who did back-breaking work as a field hand. When New York state ended slavery, she became legally free in 1827, left her country life, and settled in New York City. There she earned her living by cleaning white people's houses. During the 1830s and 1840s she took part in the great movements for social reform and religious revival. In 1843 she began a new career as a traveling preacher, spreading the word of God.

By the 1850s she was one of the nation's most famous women. She traveled from state to state, exposing the evils of slavery and championing equality for women. Nearly six feet (183 centimeters) tall, lean and strong, she was an excellent singer as well as a powerful speaker. She impressed everyone who saw or heard her.

Sojourner Truth witnessed the birth of the women's rights movement, the Civil War, and the end of slavery for African Americans. In 1864 she was welcomed to the White House by President Abraham Lincoln. And Lincoln wasn't the only president who welcomed her. She also met face-to-face with the two presidents who followed Lincoln, Andrew Johnson and Ulysses S. Grant. In Washington, D.C., the nation's capital, she fought tirelessly for the rights of African Americans to live as free people, in full equality with whites. More than 50 years before women were guaranteed the right to vote, Truth argued for women's suffrage.

Truth posed for many photos in the 1860s, when portrait photography was a new art form. She sold photos of herself to earn money in her later years.

> *I can't read a book, but I can read the people.*
> — Sojourner Truth

The Sojourner Truth Library stands on the campus of the State University of New York at New Paltz, not far from where Truth was born and raised. The three-story structure was built in 1969 and dedicated to her in 1971.

She did all these things even though she never learned how to read or write. If she wanted to send a letter, she had to speak the words to someone else, who would write them down. She told her life story to her friend Olive Gilbert, who published it in 1850 as the *Narrative of Sojourner Truth*. Truth then sold the books on her speaking tours, to raise enough money to live on.

Choosing Her Name

Sojourner Truth did not have that name when she was born. For the first half of her life she was known by the name her parents gave her—Isabella, or Belle. Choosing her own name was one of the ways she became a "self-made woman." The exact date she chose her new name was June 1, 1843. That was the day she left New York City with a couple of coins and a small bundle of clothes. She never looked back.

Why, exactly, did a middle-aged woman whose birth name was Isabella choose to call herself Sojourner Truth? A sojourner is a traveler, someone who has no permanent home. The name perfectly reflected her new career—traveling from place to place, speaking the truth to all who would listen.

The name also had a deeper religious meaning. The Bible says: "For we are strangers before [God], and sojourners, as were all our fathers: our days on the Earth are as a shadow...." (1 Chronicles 29:15). The verse means that all people are sojourners. Because all of us must die, none of us has a permanent home in the world. Our only permanent home, the Bible says, is with God.

This idea may have held special appeal to her because she was born a slave. Her ancestors had been captured and carried in slave ships from Africa to America. She was sold, like some household object, at least three times while she was growing up. Each time, she was forced to move to a new home. Even after the law said she was free, she thought of her working years in New York City as a time of bondage.

Sojourner Truth's ancestors were brought to America on slave ships. This wood engraving shows the slave ship *Wildfire*, which reached Key West, Florida, in 1860, on the eve of the Civil War. The ship began its voyage from West Africa with a cargo of about 600 slaves. By the time it reached Florida, at least 90 of them had died.

The Meaning of Truth

Choosing Truth as her name was equally important. Even in her early years, Isabella had insisted on speaking the truth. Twice she had gone to court to defend her family and her reputation. Then, as now, witnesses in court were required to swear "to tell the truth, the whole truth, and nothing but the truth."

Late in life, Sojourner told a Chicago newspaper reporter that she didn't decide on a last name until she left New York City. After taking the ferry to Long Island, she began to walk. She soon met a Quaker woman and asked for a drink of water. "What is thy name?" the Quaker woman asked. Upon hearing the answer—"Sojourner"—the

The Spirit Calls

On June 1, 1843, Sojourner Truth decided to leave New York City, where she had been living for about eight years. Here is how Olive Gilbert described that day in the *Narrative of Sojourner Truth*:

She had never been further east than the city, neither had she any friends there of whom she had particular reason to expect any thing; yet to her it was plain that her mission lay in the east, and that she would find friends there. … Having made what preparations for leaving she deemed necessary,—which was, to put up a few articles of clothing in a pillow-case, all else being deemed an unnecessary encumbrance,— about an hour before she left, she informed Mrs. Whiting, the woman of the house where she was stopping, that her name was no longer Isabella, but SOJOURNER; and that she was going east. And to her inquiry, "What are you going east for?" her answer was, "The Spirit calls me there, and I must go."

The strength, voice, and story of Sojourner Truth inspired many people to change their lives and take a stand against slavery.

woman demanded, "Sojourner what?" When Sojourner said she didn't have a last name, the woman began to make fun of her.

Sojourner left the woman and continued walking, feeling "very hot and miserable." She prayed to God to give her "a name with a handle to it." At that moment, she later told the reporter, the idea of calling herself Sojourner Truth suddenly came to her. "I was liberated," she said.

Another report gave a slightly different version of the story. In this second version, Sojourner had already chosen her last name when she met the Quaker woman. When the woman asked why she had chosen the name Truth, Sojourner answered that as a slave her last name had always been that of her master. Now, she said, she had chosen God as her master. Serving the Lord meant serving truth.

I Sell the Shadow to Support the Substance.
SOJOURNER TRUTH.

Portrait photos in the 1860s were known as "shadows." Truth had her portraits printed on cards above a caption that read: "I sell the shadow to support the substance."

Life and Legend

Many stories were told about Truth during her lifetime and after she died. Some of them were more shadow than substance. For example, one legend says she gave birth to 13 children. Historians now know she had five children, one of whom may have died very young.

Other legends surrounded her age. Posters for her speaking appearances called her the "world's oldest lecturer." At one point she even claimed she was 114 years old. When she died in 1883, some newspapers said she was 110. The writing on her tombstone says she was 105 years old when she died. This, too, was incorrect. Researchers now believe her real age at death was 86.

These legends helped turn Truth into a larger-than-life figure. Today, her wisdom, strength, and courage continue to inspire those who seek equal rights for all Americans.

Sojourner Truth died in 1883. Seven years later, her friend Frances Titus had raised enough money to have this tombstone made for her. The tombstone erroneously reports that Truth died at the age of 105.

A Continuing Inspiration

The story of Sojourner Truth has continued to inspire people, especially African American women. One of those women was Shirley Chisholm (right) of New York. In 1968 she was the first black woman to win an election to Congress. Her campaign slogan was "Unbought and Unbossed."

Four years later, she ran for president. Chisholm was the first African American—and the first woman—to make a serious bid to become the presidential choice of the Democratic Party. When she opened her campaign in April 1972, she made a point of visiting the grave site of Sojourner Truth in Battle Creek, Michigan.

CHAPTER TWO

Born into Slavery

No one wrote down the exact date or time when a slave woman living on a farm owned by Johannes Hardenbergh gave birth to a baby girl she called Isabella, or Belle. In her *Narrative*, Olive Gilbert says Isabella—who later took the name Sojourner Truth—did "not know in what year she was born." Most scholars now say she was born sometime in 1797.

A Slave in New York State

Where Belle was born is as interesting as when. Unlike the vast majority of American slaves, Belle never lived in the South. The Hardenbergh farm was located in the town

While Belle's mother was breast-feeding and caring for her baby, she would also have been expected to nurse any white babies in the Hardenbergh household.

Some of the early Dutch settlers quarreled with Native people who had been living in the Hudson River Valley of New York state for centuries. Others, like those shown here, lived in harmony with the Esopus, trading with them and working the land side-by-side.

of Hurley, Ulster County, in New York state's Hudson River Valley. The first settlers in the area had been Esopus Indians. Dutch settlers from the Netherlands arrived in the 1600s. They called their colony New Netherland.

The Dutch were slave traders and slave owners. After the British took control of New Netherland in 1664 and renamed it New York, Dutch slave owners continued to live in the Hudson River Valley. The Hardenberghs traced their history to the earliest Dutch settlers. In the middle of the 1700s, Johannes Hardenbergh owned six slaves. That made him one of the leading slave owners in Ulster County. He also owned sawmills and flour mills. Before the American Revolution, he made money trading with the Native people. During the Revolutionary War, he opposed the British and fought under General George Washington.

Belle's Family

Both of Belle's parents were born in America. Her father, a slave named James, stood tall, straight, and strong. He was known by the nickname Bomefree, which came from the Dutch word for tree. Bomefree's African ancestors on his father's side may have come from the Gold Coast, now the independent nation of Ghana. According to some 19th-century writers, Bomefree's mother was a Mohawk Indian.

Belle's mother was named Elizabeth. White adults called her Betsy, and children knew her as Mau-Mau Bett. (Mau-Mau was a Dutch version of Mama.)

The Dutch owned and traded slaves. This illustration, created by artist Howard Pyle and published in 1917, shows Dutch sailors delivering the first group of slaves to Jamestown, Virginia, in 1619. The Dutch had taken the Africans from a Spanish ship.

Her parents had come to America as slaves, probably from the Congo region of West Central Africa.

Bomefree and Betsy were two of Johannes Hardenbergh's favorite slaves. He allowed them to live in a cottage on a hilly patch of land. Most of the time they worked for him. In their spare time they grew corn, flax, and tobacco. They bought clothing and food with the money they earned from selling their crops. Young Belle grew up speaking Dutch, like her parents, and helping with the farm chores.

The Growth of Slavery in New York State

The first slaves came to New Netherland in the 1620s, soon after the Dutch colony was founded. After the British defeated the Dutch in 1664, they expanded the slave trade. During this time, the British were far harsher in dealing with slaves than the Dutch had been.

Some African Americans in New York rebelled against slavery. In 1712, for example, an armed group of 23 African Americans set fire to a slave owner's house. In the battle that followed, nine white people died. Soldiers and militia units captured 27 black people; 21 were killed, and six committed suicide. Laws passed after this uprising gave owners much more power to punish their slaves. Owners who wanted to free their slaves found it much harder to do so.

A census taken in the United States in 1790 showed that New York had more slaves than any other state in the North. The state had 25,978 African Americans, of whom 21,324 were slaves and 4,654 were free.

In addition to Belle, Betsy gave birth to at least nine children. Belle knew only one of them well—her youngest brother, Peter. The rest were all taken from their parents and sold. A five-year-old brother and three-year-old sister were taken and sold without warning when Belle was an infant.

Painful Memories

Johannes Hardenbergh died when Belle was about two years old. Unlike some slave owners, he did not provide for his slaves to be freed upon his death. Instead, he left his property—which included Bomefree, Betsy, Belle, and Peter—to his son Charles.

Charles built a large stone house, which he made into a hotel. Belle and her family were forced to give up their cottage and move into the hotel basement. The cellar was cramped and damp. Water and mud could often be seen beneath the loose floorboards.

One of the cruelest parts of slavery was the slave auction. Slave families were broken up as mothers, fathers, and children were sold to different buyers. The illustration (lower left) shows slaves being sold while a crowd of men watches. The photo (below), taken at the Green Hill Plantation in Virginia, shows a stone block and table used for displaying slaves.

After Charles Hardenbergh died, a complete listing was made of all his property. Isabella appears on page five of the list with a value of $100. Just above her on the same sheet is Belle's mother, here called Bett.

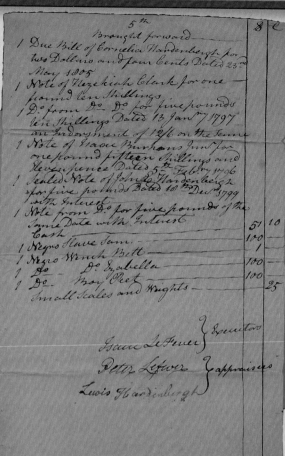

All the family members slept in the same room, with only "a little straw and a blanket" for bedding. Belle and her mother worked at the hotel from sunrise to nighttime, cooking, setting and clearing the table, cleaning the guest rooms, and doing laundry.

In "The Parting," American artist Henry Louis Stephens captured the terror and heartbreak of a slave sale. The illustration, created around 1863 as one of a series of cards depicting the life of a slave, shows a black man in chains sold to a new master, as the slave's wife and child plead to go with him.

THE PARTING "Buy us too."

"My mother, when I was sold from her, set down and wept as though her heart would break."
— Sojourner Truth

Pinkster

Life for African American slaves of Dutch families wasn't all hard work. Each year, in late May or early June, the Dutch celebrated a holiday they called Pinkster. Pinkster was the Dutch Reform version of Pentecost, the Christian religious holiday that falls seven weeks after Easter.

During Pinkster, Dutch families gave their slaves a few days off. At this time, slaves could visit with family members who had been sold to other counties. African Americans flocked to New York City, Albany, and smaller towns, where carnivals were held. Games, music, and dancing were part of the merrymaking. People competed to see who could come up with the most outrageous new dance steps. Some experts believe these were the first break dancing contests!

Modern merrymakers keep Pinkster traditions alive at an annual festival at Philipsburg Manor, in New York's Hudson River Valley. The festival includes storytelling, special foods, and performances of African-style drumming and dances.

This engraving, published in 1864, shows white masters publicly whipping and beating their slaves. Many years after her ill treatment by the Neely family, Sojourner Truth still had scars from the whippings they gave her.

Belle's life took an even more drastic turn when Charles Hardenbergh died in 1808. His holdings were divided. Belle and Peter were put up for sale. Bomefree was nearly blind, and Betsy was needed to take care of him. Both were too old to fetch a good price anyway, so they were set free and offered a hut to live in. Betsy died not long after. Bomefree lived for at least nine more years.

Showing Her Scars

Belle was purchased for $100 by John Neely, Jr., who lived near Kingston, New York. The Neelys were an English-speaking family. This immediately caused problems for Belle, whose first language was Dutch. For example, Mrs. Neely might ask her to fetch a frying pan, and she—not knowing English—would bring something else entirely. "Then, oh!, how angry mistress would be with me!" Sojourner Truth recalled. The Neelys clothed her poorly and whipped her often.

Many years later, Truth told audiences that her ill treatment by the Neely family had led her to hate white people. She would loosen her dress to show the ugly scars on her upper back. Then she would say: "When I go before the throne of God, and God says, 'Sojourner, what made you hate the white people?' I have got my answer ready."

Brutal Treatment

Isabella's sale to John Neely, Jr., marked the start of an ugly chapter in her life. In this passage from the *Narrative*, Olive Gilbert passes on Sojourner Truth's recollection of the harsh realities of her life as a slave in the Neely household:

> She was now nine years of age, and her trials in life may be dated from this period. She says, with emphasis, "Now the war *begun*." … She suffered "*terribly—terribly*" with the cold. During the winter her feet were badly frozen, for want of proper covering. They gave her a plenty to eat, and also a plenty of whippings. One Sunday morning, in particular, she was told to go to the barn; on going there, she found her master with a bundle of rods … bound together with cords. When he had tied her hands together before her, he gave her the most cruel whipping she was ever tortured with. He whipped her till the flesh was deeply lacerated, and the blood streamed from her wounds—and the scars remain to the present day.

Reflecting on her suffering at the hands of the Neelys, Sojourner Truth said: "Oh! my God! What a way is this of treating human beings?"

CHAPTER THREE

No Easy Walk to Freedom

Isabella was saved from the cruel Neely family by her father. After she had been living with the Neelys for a while, Bomefree paid her a visit. Seeing her poor condition, he began to ask some of the kinder Dutchmen he knew if one of them might be willing to buy Belle from the Neelys. At Bomefree's urging, Martimus Schryver, a Dutchman who had known the Hardenberghs, purchased Belle for $105. For John Neely, Jr., the sale meant a profit of five dollars. For Belle, leaving Neely was the answer to her prayers.

Isabella endured many personal trials and tragedies before she became famous as Sojourner Truth.

Dutch settlers built large mansions in Ulster County, New York, where Belle grew up. This Dutch colonial mansion, built in the 1700s, now serves as an inn and guest house.

A Brief, Happy Time

The Schryvers made their living by fishing and innkeeping. Belle spent much of her life outdoors, carrying fish and gathering ingredients for the beer the inn brewed and served. This happy time did not last long. Schryver had debts he could not pay, and now, this man who had never owned a slave but had bought Belle to get her away from the Neely family, was forced to sell her in order to get money. Belle was about 13 years old by this time. She was healthy and strong, had excellent household skills, and was approaching her childbearing years. Schryver found a buyer who was willing to pay about $175 for her.

With the Dumonts

Belle's new master was a landowner, John Dumont. The Dumont family came from a mixed French Protestant, Dutch, and English background. Belle lived with the Dumonts for the next 16 years—a period of enormous change in her life. Her tasks included both household and field work. Dumont was impressed with her skills, saying that Belle "could do as much work as half a dozen common [white] people, and do it well, too."

Some slaves lived in the main family home, while others lived in cabins or huts. The Hermitage Plantation, near Savannah, Georgia, had between 70 and 80 brick cabins where slaves were housed and raised for sale.

Belle became friends with Dumont's daughter Gertrude, or Getty. She viewed Belle as "uncommonly smart" and "an excellent cook."

Not everyone in the household shared that view. Dumont's wife Elizabeth, the white servants, and some of Belle's fellow slaves were jealous of Belle. They tried whenever possible to make Belle look bad. One servant named Kate, hoping to get Belle in trouble, secretly put ashes into the potatoes that Belle was cooking. After tasting the spoiled potatoes, the Dumonts scolded Belle and punished her. It was Getty who untangled the mystery. After she spied Kate trying the same trick again, Getty told her father—and everyone else in the household.

Slavery was a big business in the New World. Sugar grown by slaves in the Caribbean was shipped to New England or Europe, where it was turned into rum. The rum could then be traded or sold to buy more slaves from Africa. This hand-colored engraving (below) shows slaves at twilight, leaving the cane fields after a long day's work.

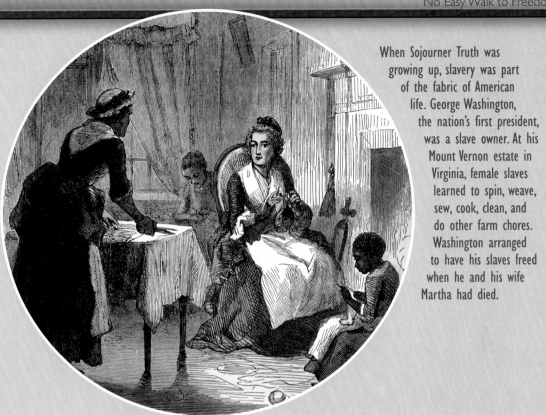

When Sojourner Truth was growing up, slavery was part of the fabric of American life. George Washington, the nation's first president, was a slave owner. At his Mount Vernon estate in Virginia, female slaves learned to spin, weave, sew, cook, clean, and do other farm chores. Washington arranged to have his slaves freed when he and his wife Martha had died.

Olive Gilbert later asked Sojourner Truth whether John Dumont had ever whipped her. Truth answered yes, he had sometimes whipped her "soundly, though never cruelly." The worst whipping he gave her, she said, was because she was cruel to a cat. Whenever he was angry with her, she worked harder and harder to win his praise. As for Dumont's wife, she continued to torment Belle at every opportunity.

Love, Marriage, and Children

During the time she lived with the Dumonts, Belle gave birth to five children. Four of them lived past infancy: Diana, Peter, Elizabeth, and Sophia. Diana was probably born about 1815. Some recent scholars believe that Diana's father was John Dumont. Others have suggested that her father was a slave called Robert, who belonged to an Englishman named Catlin or Catton. (He may have been the English painter Charles Catton, Jr., who settled in the Hudson River Valley in 1804.) Belle and Robert were in love. They wanted to be together. Catton and his son were furious at the idea. They beat Robert

Five generations belonging to the same slave family posed in 1862 for photographer Timothy O'Sullivan at Smith's Plantation, Beaufort, South Carolina. Children born to slave parents became the property of the slave owners, who could then choose to keep or sell them.

bloody when he tried to visit Belle, and ordered him to marry a servant woman in the Catton household.

Sometime later, Belle married Thomas, a slave owned by the Dumonts. He was older than she was, and had been married twice before. At least one of his earlier marriages had broken up when his wife was sold. The *Narrative of Sojourner Truth* does not say much more about Thomas or about his relationship with Belle. John Dumont's son Solomon—Getty's younger brother—recalled that Belle and Thomas had "lived unhappily together." While their marriage lasted, she gave birth to Peter in 1821 or 1822, Elizabeth in 1824 or 1825, and Sophia in 1826. As was the custom, she breast-fed her babies. She also breast-fed some of the white children among the Dumonts.

The *Narrative of Sojourner Truth* says that Belle and Thomas were not married by a minister. Instead, a fellow slave conducted the wedding. Many African American weddings ended with the ceremony of "jumping over the broom," as shown in this woodcut.

Desperate Moments

The *Narrative of Sojourner Truth* describes how Robert's owners beat him and almost killed him, while young Belle looked on in horror:

> One Saturday afternoon, hearing that Belle was ill, [Robert] took the liberty to go and see her. [The Cattons] fell upon him like tigers, beating him with the heavy ends of their canes, bruising and mangling his head and face in the most awful manner, and causing the blood, which streamed from his wounds, to cover him like a slaughtered beast. … Mr. Dumont interposed at this point, telling the ruffians they could no longer spill human blood on *his* premises—he would have "no niggers killed there." … As they led [Robert] away, like the greatest of criminals, the more humane Dumont followed them to their homes, as Robert's protector; and when he returned, he kindly went to Belle, as he called her, telling her he did not think they would strike him any more, as their wrath had greatly cooled before he left them. Isabella had witnessed this scene from her window, and was greatly shocked at the murderous treatment of poor Robert, whom she truly loved.…

THE LASH.

Some owners bound and beat their slaves bloody. Robert suffered a similar beating until John Dumont ordered Robert's owners to stop.

A New Day Dawns

Between 1790 and 1820, the slave population in the United States more than doubled, from 697,681 to 1,538,022. The opposite was true in New York state, where the number of slaves dropped from 21,324 to 10,088. The decline in New York had two main causes. First, state laws were passed that gradually required slave owners to free their slaves. Second, as the deadline approached for those laws to take effect, some New York slave owners sold their slaves to other states—especially in the South— where support for slavery remained strong.

Under a state law passed in 1817, Belle could expect to become a free woman by July 4, 1827. After she married Thomas, John Dumont made her a promise. If she continued to work hard, he pledged to free both Belle and Thomas a year early. When she heard that, she worked harder than ever. Then, she seriously injured her hand. Using the hurt hand as an excuse, Dumont broke the promise he had made to her. Belle, he said, would receive her freedom on the day the law required—and not a day sooner. Dumont also did something else that angered Belle. He sold her five-year-old son Peter to a family in New Paltz, New York. Belle was bitter. "The slave holders are TERRIBLE for promising to give you this or that, or such and such a privilege," she later complained to Olive Gilbert. "When the time of fulfillment comes, and one claims the promise, they … recollect nothing of

Like the slave woman in this woodcut, Belle had to help raise the white children in the Dumont household as well as her own.

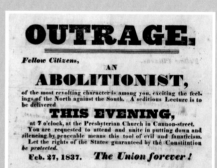

Supporters of slavery often clashed with abolitionists in the decades leading up to the Civil War. This 1837 handbill urges opponents of abolition to break up an anti-slavery meeting.

This Book tell man not to be cruel. Oh! that Issons would read this Book.

THE NEGRO WOMAN'S APPEAL

TO HER WHITE SISTERS.

Ye wives, and ye mothers, your influence extend—
Ye sisters, ye daughters, the helpless defend—
These strong ties are severed for one crime alone,
Possessing a colour less fair than your own.
Ah! why must the tints of complexion be made
A plea for the wrongs which poor Afric invade?
Alike are his children in his holy sight,
Who formed and redeems both the black and the white.
In the good book you read, I have heard it is said,
For those of all nations the Saviour has bled,—
No "respecter of persons" is he I am told,
All who love and obey him he ranks in his fold;
His laws, like himself, are both pure and divine—
Ah! why bear his name and his precepts decline.

The wounds of fresh tortures will rouse me again,
For I must not one moment forgetful remain.
My babies are crying beneath the tall trees,
Their loud sobs come borne on the soft passing breeze,
To her whose rent bosom most keenly can feel,
Though she dare not her thoughts nor her wishes reveal,
While pierced with the knowledge they're roving alone,—
No hand to conduct them, and keep them at home—
To feed them—to sooth them, and hush them to peace
On that bosom of love, where their sorrows would cease.
Their smooth glossy cheeks, which as lovely I view
As are the mixed tints of the roses to you,
Are stained with the tears I would soon kiss away,
Could I see my sweet infants the long sunny day.

Abolitionists tried to win support from white women in the North by using accounts of slave women cruelly separated from their husbands or children. Some of Sojourner Truth's leading supporters were white women such as Olive Gilbert and Harriet Beecher Stowe.

The Fight to End Slavery in New York

Abolitionists worked for decades to end the practice of slavery in New York state. In 1781 the state legislature voted to free any slaves who had fought against the British in the American Revolution. Four years later, some of the state's leading white citizens formed the New York Manumission Society. (Manumission was the legal term for giving slaves their freedom.) The group set up its first African Free School in 1787. The schools helped to train a new generation of black children.

In 1799 the legislature passed "An Act for the Gradual Abolition of Slavery." The law applied to all children born to slave women after July 4, 1799. Males would become free at age 28; females would be freed at age 25. Because Isabella was born before 1799, this law did not apply to her.

In 1817 the legislature took the final step. It passed a new law saying that by July 4, 1827, almost all slaves in New York state would have to be set free. This law did apply to Isabella and other slaves born before July 4, 1799.

John Jay was one of New York's leading opponents of slavery. He helped start the New York Manumission Society and the first African Free School. Later he became the first chief justice of the United States and the governor of New York State.

Slave owners tried many different methods to keep their slaves from running away. The unusual device demonstrated here is a bell rack found in Alabama. The bell above the slave's head was attached to a rod, which was then secured around the slave's neck and waist. If the slave left the main road and tried to run through the woods, the bell would clang as it knocked into low-hanging branches.

the kind; and you are, like as not, taunted with being a LIAR."

Belle knew she had to go. On a cool autumn morning in 1826 she awoke before dawn and crept away from the Dumont household, with a bundle of clothing in one arm and her infant daughter Sophia in the other.

By the time the Sun rose, Belle was standing alone on top of a high hill. She had left the Dumonts, her husband, and two of her daughters behind. She breathed a little easier, relieved that no one had followed her to drag her home. She did not know that her time of trials was just beginning.

No one followed Belle as she left the Dumonts. Other slaves were not so lucky. The illustration shows a man running for his life as slave hunters with a dog try to track him down.

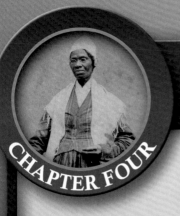
Belle's Trials

O n the day she left the Dumonts, Isabella walked about 12 miles (19 kilometers) to the home of Levi Roe, a Quaker man who opposed slavery. Roe was dying. Although he wanted to help, he was in no condition to take care of Belle and baby Sophia. He urged her to seek out a Dutch couple, Isaac and Maria Van Wagenen, who also opposed slavery. They were glad to assist.

An Act of Kindness

Not long after, John Dumont heard that Belle was with the Van Wagenens and came looking for her.

"Well, Belle," he said, "so you've run away from me."

"No, I did not *run* away," she answered.

"I walked away by daylight, and all because you had promised me a year of my time."

A close-up of the Sojourner Truth statue in Battle Creek, Michigan. The bronze figure stands 12 feet (3.66 meters) high and was created by sculptor Tina Allen.

Belle came to the courthouse in Ulster County, New York, in the late 1820s to win the return of her son Peter, who had been sold illegally to a slave owner in Alabama. The two-story stone courthouse, which was built in 1789, still serves as the hub of the Ulster County court system.

As their argument grew more intense, Isaac spoke up. He said he did not believe in slavery and "had never been in the practice of buying and selling slaves." This time was an exception. Rather than allow the angry Dumont to take Belle and Sophia, he paid $20 for Belle and $5 for her daughter.

Belle thanked Isaac for his kindness and called him "master." He would not allow it. "There is but *one* master," Isaac told her, referring to God. "And He who is *your* master is *my* master."

Rescuing Peter

While Belle was living with the Van Wagenens, Isaac brought her some alarming news. Her son Peter—now six years old—was no longer in New Paltz. His owners there had sold him, and he had been taken all the way to Alabama. New York state law clearly said that no slave could be sold to any place where slavery would still be legal after 1827. Whoever had taken Peter to Alabama had broken the law.

Belle asked the Dumonts for help. They told her no. "*Ugh!* a *fine* fuss to make about a little *nigger!*" said Elizabeth Dumont scornfully. Other people involved in selling and kidnapping Peter also refused to help get him back. To rescue Peter, Belle would have to go to court. Her chances of success did not look good. She was challenging some very powerful people. She was black and a former slave, and many people might be prejudiced against her. She had no money to pay for a lawyer. She was illiterate and therefore unable to read or write court papers.

Against these obstacles she had four things in her favor. The first three were her courage, her faith in God, and her belief in the law. The fourth was support from Quakers and others who saw her case as a way to strike another blow against slavery.

Amazingly, Belle won her case. With the aid of the New York Manumission Society, Peter was returned to New York state in 1828.

Awakenings

As Belle's situation changed, her inner life changed with it. Religion came to play a larger and larger role in her thinking. In this she was not alone. Religious revivals have been an important part of American history. The first major religious revival was called the Great Awakening. It took place in New England in the first half of the 1700s.

Names Taken Freely

Belle was about 30 years old in 1827 when she and her daughter became legally free. Grateful to Isaac and Maria Van Wagenen for making her freedom possible, she took their last name as her own. Even after she changed her name a second time—to Sojourner Truth, in 1843— she sometimes called herself Isabella Van Wagenen in legal papers.

Because it was illegal to teach slaves, Sojourner Truth never learned to read or write. This is the only known example of her signature, which she wrote in an autograph book owned by Hattie Johnson, a local high school student, on April 23, 1880.

(from the archives of the Historical Society of Battle Creek)

Sojourner Truth's only known attempt to sign her name was in a book belonging to Hattie Johnson, a Michigan schoolgirl. Truth signed Johnson's autograph book in 1880. The signature is reproduced in a plaque on the wall of the Sojourner Truth Library in New Paltz, New York.

The Second Great Awakening began after the American Revolution and gathered force during the early decades of the 1800s. Preachers traveled from place to place, speaking at camp meetings to hundreds or even thousands of excited listeners. People at a camp meeting didn't just sit quietly and listen. They clapped, shouted, sang, and danced. Some even fell to the ground, overcome with emotion. Many of these traveling preachers taught that everyone—white or black—was equal in the sight of God. The Second Great Awakening helped open people's eyes to the evils of slavery. It helped convert people to the abolitionist cause.

Methodism was one of the fastest-growing religions during this period. Methodist preachers traveled around the country on horseback. They taught that anyone who had faith in Jesus and gave up sin could be saved.

Belle began attending and preaching at camp meetings in the late 1820s. At a typical camp meeting, traveling preachers would speak to large crowds every few hours. The times in between were filled with praying, singing, hand clapping, and other expressions of religious fervor. These illustrations show a typical meeting (top) and a view of the tents on the meeting grounds (bottom).

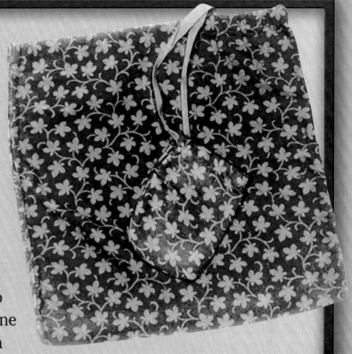

For much of her life, Sojourner Truth smoked a pipe. She kept her tobacco in this pouch, which is now held by the Michigan Historical Museum in Lansing, Michigan.

They preached against loose behavior and public drunkenness. While she lived with the Van Wagenens, Belle began attending Methodist camp meetings. In 1827, around the time of the Pinkster holiday, she had a powerful experience in which she felt the presence of Jesus. She decided to change her ways. According to Getty Dumont, Belle had been "fond of liquor and tobacco, and used both when she could get them … but she became greatly changed in these respects afterwards."

In the Kingdom of Matthias

In the autumn of 1828, Belle left the Van Wagenens and moved, along with Peter, to New York City. Methodist friends provided her with contacts, and she soon found work in the households of Methodist families. For two years she worked for James and Cornelia La Tourette. James was a fur merchant who had also gained a following as a Methodist preacher. Belle preached at camp meetings she attended with the La Tourettes. She also worshiped at the John Street Methodist Church in lower Manhattan.

Belle next worked as a live-in housekeeper for the preacher and social reformer Elijah Pierson. Pierson's religious views were extreme. When his wife Sarah died, he was sure that if he prayed hard enough at her funeral, she would come back to life. Months later, he continued to believe—falsely, as it turned out—that Sarah would return to him from the dead.

Belle was at the Pierson home on May 5, 1832, when a man named Robert Matthews appeared at the door. He was tall and thin, with piercing eyes, long hair, and a full beard. Belle's first thought was that he looked like Jesus. He called himself Matthias the Prophet. Matthias managed to convince Pierson, Belle, and others that he had come to establish the Kingdom of God on Earth. Belle gave her money to Matthias. Others did, too.

In 1833, Matthias and his followers moved from New York City to a farm in Westchester County.

Noisy celebrations greeted Independence Day in New York City on July 4, 1834. By this time, Belle had left the city to live at Zion Hill in Westchester County.

One of the places where Belle worshiped was the John Street Methodist Church in New York City. A Methodist church has stood on this site since 1768. The church building shown here opened its doors in 1841 and is still used today.

They named their new home Zion Hill, or the Kingdom of Matthias. Here everyone was supposed to be equal. They weren't. Belle—the only black woman among the followers—did much of the housework. Matthias ruled his "kingdom" like the leader of a cult. Rumors of strange behavior by the leader and his followers began to reach the outside world.

The Kingdom of Matthias collapsed when Elijah Pierson became sick in late July 1834 after eating two plates of blackberries. Matthias refused to call a doctor. Only prayer, he said, could cure Pierson's illness. When Pierson died in early August, newspaper reports accused Matthias of being a scoundrel and possibly a murderer. Some people even accused Belle of plotting to poison Pierson.

Belle insisted she was innocent. As she said,

> *I have got the truth and I know it, and I will crush them with the truth.*

In the 1800s, traveling Methodist preachers—known as circuit riders—rode from town to town on horseback. This magazine cover from 1887 shows a Methodist circuit rider braving a rainstorm.

She was right. With help from friends, she was able to clear her name. A British writer published a book telling her side of the story.

For the second time in seven years she went to court. She sued one of her accusers, Benjamin Folger, who had also been part of the Kingdom of Matthias. She won her court case, and Folger had to pay her $125.

Mission of Truth

In 1835, Belle returned to New York City. For the next eight years she did household work. She suffered a number of setbacks during this period. A steep economic downturn began in 1837, and the hard times lasted for another five years. Worries about her son Peter were a heavy weight on her spirits. She told Olive Gilbert she felt "that every thing she had undertaken in the city of New York had finally proved a failure; and where her hopes had been raised the highest, there she felt the failure had been the greatest, and the disappointment most severe."

Many Americans were becoming anxious. Some preachers claimed the world would end soon. Repent, they said, because Judgment Day was coming.

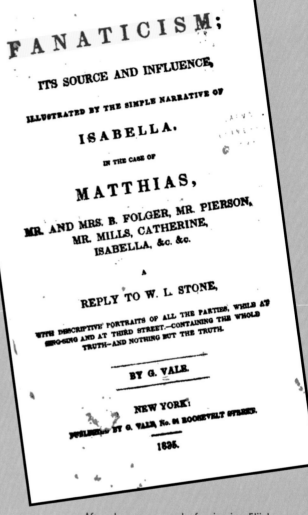

After she was accused of poisoning Elijah Pierson, Belle answered her critics in this book, which was published in 1835. The author, Gilbert Vale, was an Englishman who left London for New York City in 1829. One bond that united Belle and Vale was their opposition to slavery.

Lost at Sea

Peter's story does not have a happy ending. As a young boy growing up in Ulster County, New York, he had a reputation as a troublemaker. He had problems getting and holding a job, and he gambled away his earnings. Given the chance to attend school, he showed little interest. He was arrested several times for stealing. Friends of Belle's may have kept him from going to prison.

In 1839, Peter signed on as a sailor on the whaling ship *Zone*. It sailed from Massachusetts in May. In a letter written from sea in 1840, he asked his mother to forgive him "for all that I have done." The last letter she received from him was dated September 19, 1841. The ship returned home without him in May 1843. She never heard from him again. Why did Peter fail to return? Some writers think he may have lost his life because of a mutiny. Others say he may have died when an outbreak of smallpox hit the ship. An accident at sea is a third possibility. No one knows for sure.

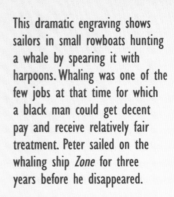

This dramatic engraving shows sailors in small rowboats hunting a whale by spearing it with harpoons. Whaling was one of the few jobs at that time for which a black man could get decent pay and receive relatively fair treatment. Peter sailed on the whaling ship *Zone* for three years before he disappeared.

One preacher, William Miller, even said he knew the exact date when the world would end—March 21, 1843. (When it didn't happen, he changed his prediction to March 21, 1844.)

Belle was less concerned with the exact date than with the need to do something meaningful with her life. She knew slavery was evil. She had the scars to prove it. She knew women deserved equal rights with men. She had courage and strength that were equal to any man's. When she left New York City on June 1, 1843, with only a small bundle of belongings and the clothes on her back, she was a woman on a mission. She would travel from camp meeting to camp meeting, speaking out against slavery and standing up for women's rights. She would speak the truth to all who were willing to listen.

Her life as Isabella was over. For this new mission she took a new name—Sojourner Truth.

A statue of a woman in chains, part of a slave memorial on the African island of Zanzibar. The island was the site of a slave market in which many thousands of African men, women, and children were treated like prisoners and sold like cattle.

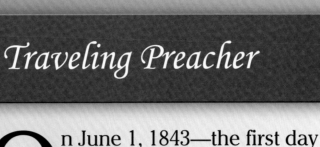

CHAPTER FIVE

Traveling Preacher

On June 1, 1843—the first day of her new life with her new name— Sojourner Truth headed east to Long Island. Day after day, week after week, she walked from town to town, preaching wherever she could and earning money by cooking and doing other odd jobs. Many of her early hearers were followers of William Miller. These "Millerites" believed that people needed to repent right away because Jesus was coming to punish the wicked and reward the good.

Tina Allen's statue of Sojourner Truth at Battle Creek shows her with one hand on the Bible. Truth, who was illiterate, could not read the Bible herself. Instead, she liked to have children read the Bible to her.

As the months passed, excitement grew about this tall black woman with a gift for preaching and singing. People who heard her recommended her to friends in other towns. Soon she was attracting large crowds in Connecticut and Massachusetts.

The Northampton Association

In 1844, Sojourner Truth's friends urged her to come to Northampton, in western Massachusetts. Extraordinary things were happening there. Two years earlier, a small group of men had founded the Northampton Association of Education and Industry. These men (and the dozens of people who soon joined them) all agreed on some basic ideas. They opposed slavery. They favored equal treatment for all people—whites and blacks, old and young, women and men, rich and poor. They supported education for girls as well as boys. They believed in the Second Great Awakening and prayed for a religious revival. They wanted to live together in harmony as a community.

William Lloyd Garrison, a leading abolitionist, visited Northampton while Truth was living there. She probably met him in 1844.

In time, the Northampton Association had more than 200 members. To earn money, they made and sold silk. The group became a center of anti-slavery activity. Leading abolitionists such as William Lloyd Garrison and Frederick Douglass came there.

In a pencil drawing made around 1867, the artist Charles Burleigh showed Truth bending over a washtub, doing laundry at Northampton.

Douglass, a former slave, wrote that the "place and the people struck me as the most democratic I had ever met. … There was no high, no low, no masters, no servants, no white, no black. I, however, felt myself in very high society."

Sojourner Truth fit right in. Her job was to run the laundry. She also became one of the group's moral leaders. She learned from her contact with well-educated people who had forward-looking ideas. She sharpened her own views about slavery and women's rights. She also enjoyed the company of her daughters Sophia and Elizabeth, who came to live with her.

Quieting an Angry Mob

One evening in 1844, Sojourner Truth learned just how powerfully her voice could affect all who heard it. A few months after she arrived at Northampton, Massachusetts, she attended a large camp meeting. A band of "wild young men" began "hooting and yelling," trying to disrupt the preaching and praying. Sojourner Truth was the only African American at the camp meeting. In the *Narrative*, she admits that she was afraid the angry white men might attack or even kill her.

Her first impulse was to hide. Then her faith and courage returned to her. In the bright moonlight, she climbed atop a small hill and began singing a hymn as loudly as she could.

The mob approached her, carrying weapons in their hands. Gently but firmly she said, "Why do you come about me with clubs and sticks? I am not doing harm to any one." "We ar'n't a going to hurt you, old woman," they answered. Other voices cried out, "Sing to us, old woman" and "Talk to us, old woman." She sang, spoke, and prayed with them for an hour, and they left in peace.

SOJOURNER'S MIRROR.

AIR—"AULD LANG SYNE."

Sojourner Truth,

Interested an audience in New Lisbon, Ohio, at the Methodist Episcopal Church, very much, for near an hour, in talking of slavery in this country, and the suffering and injustice inseparable from it. If earnestness is eloquence—and it is—she has a just claim in that appellation, for she makes some powerful appeals which cannot but strike a chord of sympathy in every human heart.

A friend who was present addressed the following lines to the Editor of the *Aurora*.

She pleadeth for her people,
A poor, down-trodden race,
Who dwell in Freedom's boasted land,
With no abiding place.

She pleadeth that her people
May have their rights restored,
For they have long been toiling,
And yet had no reward.

They are forced the crops to culture,
But not for them they yield,
Although both late and early
They labor in the field.

While she hears upon her body
The scars of many a gash,
She pleadeth for her people
That groan beneath the lash.

She impleading for the mothers
Who gaze in wild despair
Upon the hated auction-block,
And see their children there.

She feels for those in bondage—

But while your kindest sympathies
To foreign lands do roam,
She would ask you to remember
Your own oppressed at home.
She pleads with you to sympathise
With sighs, and groans, and scars,
And note how base the tyranny
Beneath the stripes and stars.

Sojourner's Favorite Song.

We are going home, we have visions bright
Of that holy land, that world of light
Where the long dark night is past,
And the morning of eternity has come at last,
Where the weary Saints no more shall roam,
But dwell in a sunny, and peaceful home,
Where the brow, celestial gems shall crown
And waves of bliss are dashing 'round.

Chorus—Oh! that beautiful home—oh! that beautiful world.

We are going home, we soon shall be
Where the sky is clear and the soil is free,
Where the victor's song floats over the plains,
And the Seraphs anthem blends with the strains,
Where the sun rolls down his brilliant flood
And beams on a world all fair and good,
And the stars that shone on nature's dome
Will sparkle and dance o'er the spirits home.

Chorus.

The tears and sighs, which here were given,
Exchanged for the glad songs of heaven,
The beauteous forms that sing and shine
And guarded well, by a hand divine,
Pure love and friendship joined.

Truth was famous for her songs as well as her preaching. She set new words to familiar tunes such as "Auld Lang Syne."

41

As the years passed, Truth's fame spread, and more and more people came to hear her. After each lecture, she raised money by selling song sheets, copies of the *Narrative*, or photos of herself.

FREE LECTURE!
SOJOURNER TRUTH,

Who has been a slave in the State of New York, and who has been a Lecturer for the last twenty-three years, whose characteristics have been so vividly portrayed by Mrs. Harriet Beecher Stowe, as the African Nybil, will deliver a lecture upon the present issues of the day,

On

At

And will give her experience as a Slave mother and religious woman. She comes highly recommended as a public speaker, having the approval of many thousands who have heard her earnest appeals, among whom are Wendell Phillips, Wm. Lloyd Garrison, and other distinguished men of the nation.

☞ At the close of her discourse she will offer for sale her photograph and a few of her choice songs.

Her Fame Grows

During this period, Truth became friends with Olive Gilbert. Gilbert, a white woman, was born in Connecticut in 1801. She hated slavery, which she had seen up close while visiting her brother in Kentucky. Gilbert and Truth were living in Northampton in 1845 when the *Narrative of the Life of Frederick Douglass, An American Slave* appeared. Douglass's book sold very well. Impressed by his success, Gilbert began working with Truth on her own slave story. The *Narrative of Sojourner Truth* was published in 1850. Money from the book helped Truth buy a house in the Northampton area.

Sojourner Truth's fame increased rapidly in the early 1850s. Many people were attracted to her unusual gifts as a preacher, speaker, and singer. She was unusual in other ways as well. She was much taller than most women of that time. Her voice was much deeper, too. Unlike most slaves, she had lived in the North her whole life. When she spoke at anti-slavery rallies, she was often the only black woman on the platform.

People were amazed when they learned that, although she could speak words of great power and wisdom, she could not read or write. Her lack of education became part of her legend. Many people who heard her felt that God was speaking to them *through* her.

"And Ar'n't I a Woman?"

Something else unusual about Sojourner Truth was that as a black woman she spoke both as an abolitionist and a feminist. Abolitionists in

The Story of a Book

Sojourner Truth was about 53 years old when her *Narrative* was published in 1850 in Boston. The book sold for 25 cents a copy and told her story through 1849. It must have been popular, because more copies were printed in New York City that same year.

NARRATIVE
OF
SOJOURNER TRUTH,
A
NORTHERN SLAVE,
EMANCIPATED FROM BODILY SERVITUDE BY THE STATE OF
NEW YORK, IN 1828.

WITH A PORTRAIT.

BOSTON:
PRINTED FOR THE AUTHOR.
1850.

SOJOURNER TRUTH.

In 1852, Harriet Beecher Stowe published the anti-slavery novel *Uncle Tom's Cabin*. The book made Stowe world famous. Hoping to boost sales of the *Narrative*, Truth met with Stowe and asked for her help. Stowe agreed. Her support helped Truth become known throughout the United States.

A new edition of the *Narrative* appeared in 1875, when Truth was nearly 80 years old. This much larger book was prepared by Truth's friend Frances Titus. It included letters to Truth and articles about her. Titus also prepared the 1884 edition of the *Narrative*. It appeared after Truth's death and included tributes to her and an account of her funeral.

Shown above: The 1850 edition of Sojourner Truth's *Narrative*. An expanded edition was published in 1875. That version included selections from Truth's notebooks, which she called her "Book of Life." Because Truth could not read, she trusted Frances Titus to make the selections for her.

Left: Frances Titus lived in Battle Creek. She first met Sojourner Truth in the mid-1850s, and they began working closely together in the 1870s. Like Truth, Titus was a strong supporter of equal rights for women and for African Americans.

America had been fighting against slavery for decades. The campaign for women's rights was much more recent. The first Women's Rights Convention was held in 1848 at Seneca Falls, New York. Lucretia Mott was one of the organizers of that meeting, at which Frederick Douglass also spoke. In 1850, Truth joined Mott and Douglass at another women's rights convention, in Worcester, Massachusetts.

A year later, Truth gave one of the most important speeches of her

Sojourner Truth posed for this famous photo (above, right) in 1864. The feminist leader Susan B. Anthony used copies of this picture to help raise money for women's rights.

This "Portrait Monument" honoring three leaders in the fight for women's rights (left) stands in the U.S. Capitol in Washington, D.C. The marble sculpture, by Adelaide Johnson, shows (from left to right) Elizabeth Cady Stanton, Susan B. Anthony, and Lucretia Mott.

life at the Ohio Woman's Rights Convention, in Akron. There are two versions of this speech. The first was reported by her friend Marius Robinson not long after she delivered it. In this version she said:

> *I have as much muscle as any man, and can do as much work as any man. I have plowed and reaped and husked and chopped and mowed, and can any man do more than that? I have heard much about the sexes being equal; I can carry as much as any man, and can eat as much too, if I can get it. I am as strong as any man that is now.*

Truth also dealt with the argument, made by some people, that men were naturally smarter than women. She answered that even if men really were smarter, women still had a right to a good education. Robinson's report put her reply this way: "As for intellect, all I can say is, if a woman have a pint and a man a quart—why can't she have her little pint full?"

A second version of this speech appeared in 1863. It was written by Frances Dana Gage, an organizer of the Women's Rights Convention in Akron. Her report has Truth speaking in a thick southern Negro dialect. In Gage's version, Truth says again and again, in a voice like rolling thunder, "And ar'n't I a woman?" Gage also has Truth claiming she gave birth to 13 children "and seen 'em mos' all sold off the slavery."

In one published version of her Ohio speech, Truth asks again and again, "And ar'n't I a woman?" Today, many historians think she may never have said these words at all. The quotation may actually have come from an earlier source: a picture in the book *Slavery Illustrated in Its Effects upon Woman and Domestic Society*, which appeared in 1837. One version of that picture, published in William Lloyd Garrison's abolitionist newspaper *The Liberator*, is shown here.

'Am I not a Woman and a Sister?'

Robinson's article—which recent scholars think is more accurate—was lost for many decades. Truth's speech survived in Gage's version. Feminists in the 1960s and 1970s who were inspired by Truth read her speech as Gage had reported it. Did she actually say "And ar'n't I a woman?" No one knows for sure whether these well-known words connected with Truth are fact or legend.

A Disagreement with Douglass

Another well-known story about Truth concerns an argument she had with Frederick Douglass. The two former slaves attended an anti-slavery convention in 1852 in Salem, Ohio. At this time, opponents of slavery were deeply divided over how slaves could best gain their freedom.

One group said the only good way was to persuade white slave owners that slavery was wrong.

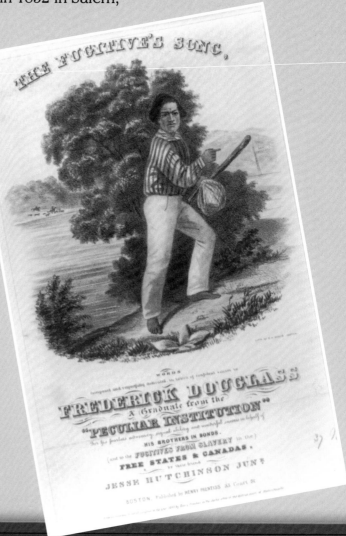

Sojourner Truth and Frederick Douglass knew each other for about 40 years. Both had been slaves, and both were tireless opponents of slavery. This song sheet (right) pictures Douglass as a runaway slave. The photo (facing page) offers a formal portrait from his later years.

46

These abolitionists opposed the use of violence to end slavery. They believed that, with God's help, the slave owners would come to see the error of their ways. A second group of abolitionists warned that violence might be needed. They said that if slave owners kept mistreating slaves, the slaves had the right to fight back.

The convention hall was packed. Speakers made strong arguments on both sides. Now it was Douglass's turn to address the crowd. For most of his career, he had opposed using violent methods in the fight against slavery. Recently, his views had begun to change. There were times, he said, when just trying to persuade people wasn't enough. In extreme cases, change might require "shedding of the blood of tyrants."

Shaming Her Critics

Sojourner Truth was so tall, and her voice was so deep and powerful, that some white critics accused her of being a man. These critics, who were defenders of slavery, didn't want people to pay attention to what Truth had to say. Instead, they hoped to shame Truth into keeping quiet— or force her to admit she was lying about her gender.

Truth attacked her critics head-on at a meeting in Indiana in 1858. One man demanded that she prove she was a woman by showing her breast to the women who were there. "Sojourner told them that her breasts had suckled many a white babe," an abolitionist newspaper reported. She said that she had nothing to be ashamed of, and that she would show her breast to the whole audience, not just the women. And she did!

Hearing his words, Sojourner Truth cried out, "Is God *gone*?" The crowd was stunned. They understood what she meant. Slavery was evil, and so was violence. If people still trusted God to make things better, they did not need to use evil methods to end slavery.

This story, like others about Truth, took on a life of its own. Harriet Beecher Stowe retold it in an article she wrote in 1863. In Stowe's version Truth said, "Frederick, *is God dead*?" This is the way the story was told for many decades. The words "Is God Dead?" even appeared on her tombstone—the same stone that claimed, wrongly, that she died at the age of 105!

Harriet Beecher Stowe gained worldwide fame when she published her anti-slavery novel *Uncle Tom's Cabin* in the early 1850s. Stowe admired Sojourner Truth and helped spread Truth's message—along with a few stories about Truth that turned out to be legend rather than fact.

Not everyone shared Sojourner Truth's belief in nonviolence. In 1831, Nat Turner (left) led a slave revolt in Virginia. Turner and more than 40 followers killed at least 55 white people. He was captured, tried, and hanged, and his followers were also killed. Sadly, the rebellion sparked further violence, as angry white mobs murdered many African Americans who had nothing to do with Turner's uprising.

An Honor for Truth

Today, Seneca Falls is the home of the National Women's Hall of Fame. Sojourner Truth was inducted into the Hall of Fame in 1981. Lucretia Mott and Harriet Beecher Stowe are also members.

CHAPTER SIX

The Final Years

Sojourner Truth continued to speak out against slavery throughout the 1850s. In 1856 she was invited to come to Battle Creek, Michigan. The abolitionist movement was active in Battle Creek. The town was an important stop on the Underground Railroad that helped slaves escape to freedom in Canada. Friends of hers had bought land near Battle Creek and set up a farm community called Harmonia. Members of the community were committed to the ideals of harmony, love, and justice.

The Underground Railroad was a network of people opposed to slavery who helped slaves escape to freedom. This historic painting, completed in the early 1890s by Charles T. Webber, shows anti-slavery activists helping runaway slaves in Cincinnati, Ohio.

A New Home

Truth liked what she saw. She sold her home in Northampton, Massachusetts, and moved to Harmonia in 1857. Over time, her daughters Diana and Elizabeth and other family members also settled there. Truth made her home near Battle Creek for the last 26 years of her life.

A statue on Goree Island, Senegal, recalls the era when millions of slaves left Africa in chains. Senegal is now a free country in West Africa.

Making Freedom Real

When the Civil War broke out in 1861, Truth was more than 60 years old. She supported the Union against the South, hoping the war would speed the day when slaves would be free. She continued to work hard, even as her health failed. Friends feared she might not live much longer. They were amazed when, in the spring of 1863, she began to recover. "It is the mind that makes the body," she said. "New ideas, new thoughts bring a new mind and renew the whole system."

Truth had good reason to feel hopeful. In April 1862, President Abraham Lincoln signed a law ending slavery in Washington, D.C. By summer, freed slaves—then known as freedmen—were flooding into the nation's capital. In September, Lincoln's Emancipation Proclamation became public. As of January 1, 1863, it freed the slaves in any area that was still waging war against the Union. It did not free all the slaves. It did not go as far as the abolitionists wanted. Sojourner Truth knew all this—and celebrated anyway. She believed that God had chosen Lincoln to free her people.

Diana Corbin (top right) was the oldest of Truth's children and the one who lived the longest. She died in 1904 and was buried near her mother in Battle Creek, Michigan. The illustration of Truth (right) shows the resemblance between mother and daughter.

She had a special reason to feel proud in the spring of 1863. Northern states had begun accepting black soldiers to fight for the Union. Her grandson James signed up to fight as part of a Massachusetts regiment.

About 160,000 African Americans joined the Union Army to fight in the Civil War. This photo shows men of the 4th U.S. Colored Infantry, based in Washington, D.C. Most of the men actually came from Connecticut, and they fought in South Carolina.

The "Book of Life"

As she traveled around the country, Sojourner Truth kept several notebooks with her. She called them her "Book of Life." Whenever she met important people, she would ask for their autograph. The notebooks also included articles about her and encouraging words from her friends and supporters. Among those who signed were Abraham Lincoln, William Lloyd Garrison, Lucretia Mott, and Susan B. Anthony. Selections from the "Book of Life" were published alongside the *Narrative* beginning in 1875.

President Abraham Lincoln signed Sojourner Truth's "Book of Life" when the two met at the White House in 1864.

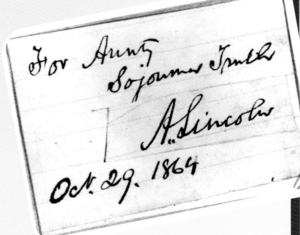

Truth and the Presidents

In 1864, Truth felt well enough to travel all the way from Michigan to Washington, D.C. She had two reasons for making the trip. She wanted to meet President Lincoln, and she wanted to help the freedmen. Truth got her first wish on October 29. She entered the White House at 8:00 A.M. She had to wait for hours while Lincoln talked with many other people, both white and black. "I appreciate you, for you are the best president who has ever taken the seat,"

she told him. He showed her a beautiful Bible "the colored people of Baltimore" had given him to thank him for issuing the Emancipation Proclamation. Then, at her request, he signed his name in one of her notebooks. "For Aunty Sojourner Truth," he wrote, and signed it "A. Lincoln."

After Lincoln was shot and killed in April 1865, Andrew Johnson became president. Truth met him, too. Their meeting was short. She told a friend "there was not much to him." A few years later she visited a third president, Ulysses S. Grant. Grant had been the Union's top general in the

This painting by Franklin C. Courter shows the meeting between Truth and Lincoln in 1864. The artist focused on the moment when Lincoln showed Truth a Bible that had been given to him by the African-American community in Baltimore, Maryland. Courter's painting was first shown to the public in 1893. It was later destroyed in a fire, and only a photo of it survives.

Civil War. Truth campaigned for him when he ran for president in 1868. When she came to the White House to see him, he greeted her warmly. He bought one of her photos for five dollars and signed his name in her book.

Aiding the Freedmen

Truth spent most of her time from late 1864 through 1868 helping the freedmen. Many thousands of black men and women had come to Washington, D.C. Most of them were desperately poor. They lacked food, clothing, shelter, and medical care. Truth worked for the National Freedman's Relief Association, a private group. She also worked for the Freedmen's Bureau, a government agency. She nursed the sick, helped the homeless, and found food for the hungry. She also taught former slaves

Sojourner and the Streetcars

When Sojourner Truth came to Washington in 1864, the city had a system of horse-drawn streetcars. The law said that African Americans had the right to ride in streetcars alongside white people. White streetcar operators often disobeyed this law. They would speed past black customers, pretending not to see them.

Truth would have none of this. Sometimes she would use her huge voice to bellow "I WANT TO RIDE!!!" At other times, she would try to run alongside the car and jump on board before anyone could stop her. This was risky. One conductor pushed her off a streetcar, injuring Truth's shoulder. She went to court to make sure the conductor was punished.

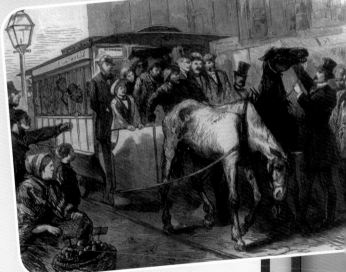

Sojourner Truth demanded that streetcar drivers and conductors treat African Americans fairly.

In April 2009, Sojourner Truth became the first black woman to have her statue put on display at the U.S. Capitol in Washington, D.C. Celebrating the occasion were U.S. First Lady Michelle Obama (left) and sculptor Artis Lane, who created the work.

from the South some of the things they needed to know about life in the North.

Throughout the South, freed slaves were having a hard time. They had no money and no jobs. Truth believed they deserved a fresh start. She wanted the United States to offer freedmen cheap land in the West. She asked the government to organize a mass movement of freed blacks to settle the frontier. This did not happen. Instead, some southern African Americans began to head westward on their own. They began this movement in the late 1870s.

In the mid-1860s, right after the Civil War, new laws in southern states had made life extremely difficult for freed blacks. These laws, known as the "Black Codes," were passed with the purpose of restricting such basic civil rights as the rights to assemble, testify in court, and carry firearms. By the late 1870s, most of those same southern states passed laws restricting the rights of black people to vote.

The United States Postal Service issued a stamp honoring Truth in 1986.

In addition to being hurt by these laws, African Americans lost political power through violence and intimidation directed at them by white groups that were determined to keep black people from showing up at the ballot box and casting their votes.

Many freedmen feared they might become slaves again. In 1879 alone, about 15,000 African Americans left the South and headed west to Kansas. They called themselves Exodusters. The name came from Exodus, a book of the Bible. The book of Exodus tells how the ancient Hebrews escaped from slavery and journeyed to the Promised Land. Truth called the Exodusters "the greatest movement of all time." She traveled to Kansas in 1879 to help the new arrivals.

Out of This World

More than 120 years have passed since the death of Sojourner Truth. In that time, there have been many tributes to her memory. One of the most unusual came in 1997 from the National Aeronautics and Space Administration. To mark the 200th anniversary of her birth, NASA launched a small, six-wheeled robot vehicle named Sojourner. The Mars Pathfinder spacecraft carried Sojourner on its long journey through space. The rover then landed on Mars and began exploring the planet's surface.

NASA wanted to name the rover after a woman who was important in history. The space agency conducted a worldwide contest in which students were asked to select a heroine and write an essay about her achievements. Nearly 1,700 essays were submitted by students between the ages of five and 18. Valerie Ambroise, a 12-year-old student from Connecticut, sent in the winning entry about Sojourner Truth.

A robot rover named to honor Sojourner Truth explored the planet Mars in 1997. The rover's camera sent 550 images of the Martian surface back to Earth.

Remembering Truth

Truth spent her last years in the Battle Creek area. There and elsewhere, she was a beloved figure. By now she was more than 80 years old and had painful sores on her legs. Despite her age and declining health, she continued to give speeches in southern Michigan. She campaigned, as always, for the rights of women. She also spoke out for temperance (the movement against the sale and consumption of alcoholic beverages) and against the death penalty.

Her condition took a turn for the worse in late 1882. During her final months, her daughters Diana and Elizabeth took care of her. She died on November 26, 1883, at 3:00 A.M. About a thousand people went to her funeral. Fond tributes poured in from many people who had worked with her to abolish slavery. "She has been for the last forty years an object of respect and admiration for social reformers everywhere," wrote Frederick Douglass.

The abolitionist Wendell Phillips was even more heartfelt. He called her a "remarkable person" and described her speaking style as "rich, quaint, poetic, and often profound." He ended with one of her favorite sayings: "You read books; God himself talks to me."

This large mural stands nearly 20 feet (6 meters) high and decorates the Sojourner Truth Library in New Paltz, New York. Art education teacher Rikki Asher and 13 of her students created the work in 1995.

Chronology

c. 1797 James and Elizabeth—two slaves living in Hurley, Ulster County, New York—have a daughter, whom they call Isabella, or Belle.

c. 1808 John Neely, Jr., an Englishman, buys Belle for $100. After he mistreats her, she is sold to Martimus Schryver for $105.

1810 John Dumont purchases her for about $175. She lives with the Dumont family for about 16 years.

c. 1815–1826 Belle gives birth to five children, at least three of them while married to Thomas, another slave owned by the Dumonts.

1826 Belle's son Peter is sold. Taking her infant daughter Sophia, she leaves the Dumont family a year before she becomes legally free. She begins working for the Van Wagenen family in Hurley, New York.

1827 Slaves are officially freed under New York state law.

1828 After her son Peter is illegally sold to a slave owner in Alabama, Belle goes to court and wins him back. With Peter, she moves to New York City.

1832 While working in the home of Elijah Pierson, Belle meets Robert Matthews, who calls himself Matthias the Prophet. She and Pierson join his followers.

1834–1835 The "Kingdom of Matthias" in Westchester County collapses after Pierson dies. Accused of plotting to poison Pierson, Belle wins a court fight to clear her name.

1835–43 She lives in New York City, earning her living by doing household work. In 1839, Peter heads out to sea on a whaling ship and never returns.

1843 On June 1, Belle changes her name to Sojourner Truth and leaves New York City. She launches a career as a traveling preacher, speaking against slavery and in favor of women's rights.

1844–1845 As part of the Northampton Association, in western Massachusetts, she meets many abolitionist leaders.

1850 Olive Gilbert publishes the *Narrative of Sojourner Truth*.

1851 She gives her most famous speech at a women's rights convention in Akron, Ohio.

1857 Truth buys a house near Battle Creek, Michigan.

1861–1865 The Civil War brings an end to slavery in the United States.

1864 Truth meets President Abraham Lincoln at the White House. In Washington, D.C., she helps freed African Americans from the South.

1870-1872 She campaigns to build support for a plan to settle freed slaves on land in the West.

1879 Thousands of Exodusters stream into Kansas. She travels to Kansas to help them.

1883 Truth dies in Battle Creek, Michigan, on November 26.

1981 Nearly a century after her death, she is inducted into the National Women's Hall of Fame in Seneca Falls, New York.

1997 A space probe named Sojourner in her honor explores the surface of the planet Mars.

2009 With First Lady Michelle Obama in attendance, a statue of Truth is unveiled at the U.S. Capitol in Washington, D.C.

Glossary

abolitionist Someone who calls for an end to a particular practice, especially slavery.

autograph A person's own signature; an example of handwriting, often by someone famous.

bondage Slavery, or any condition that feels like it.

camp meeting A large religious revival meeting, held outdoors or in a tent.

census An official count of the number of people living in a particular area.

Civil War A war fought from 1861 to 1865 between the northern and southern states. It began when the South (or Confederacy) rebelled against the Union. The war, which was won by the North, brought an end to slavery in the United States.

colony An area settled and controlled by people from another country.

conductor The person in charge of a public streetcar or train.

convention A large meeting or conference.

dialect The distinct version of a language as it is spoken in a particular region or by a specific social group.

Emancipation Proclamation An order issued by President Abraham Lincoln during the Civil War. The order freed the slaves on January 1, 1863, in any area that was still rebelling against the Union.

encumbrance A burden.

Exodusters The freed blacks who fled the South in large numbers to settle in Kansas in the late 1870s.

feminist A person who supports women's rights; someone who champions political, social, and economic equality for women.

freedmen Term used in the 1800s for slaves who had been freed; now sometimes called freedpeople or freedpersons.

Great Awakening A period of religious revival that began in New England in the mid-1700s. See also *Second Great Awakening*.

illiterate Unable to read or write.

inquiry A question.

interposed Got in the way; intervened.

Judgment Day In some religious traditions, the end of the world, when good people will be rewarded and evildoers punished.

lacerated Deeply cut; wounded.

legislature The branch of government that has the power to make laws; a group of people elected or chosen for that purpose.

liberated Freed.

manumission In law, a term for giving slaves their freedom.

militia A fighting force consisting of ordinary citizens rather than full-time soldiers.

National Aeronautics and Space Administration The official space agency of the United States government; often called NASA.

New England In the northeastern United States, a region that includes Connecticut, Massachusetts, Rhode Island, Vermont, New Hampshire, and Maine.

Pinkster A holiday celebrated by the Dutch seven weeks after Easter; slaves got a few days off, which they used for merrymaking with family and friends.

recollect Recall; remember.

regiment A unit of the armed forces.

repent Express sincere regret for bad behavior and promise to do better.

ruffians Thugs; brutes.

scholars Researchers; experts.

Second Great Awakening A period of religious revival that began after the American Revolution and lasted through the first half of the 1800s.

sojourner A traveler; a person who has no permanent home.

suffrage The right to vote in elections for public office.

temperance A movement to limit or ban the drinking of alcoholic beverages.

tyrants People who use cruelty and violence to control others.

Underground Railroad The secret network of people who helped slaves escape from the South to the North and then across the border into Canada.

THE PARTING "Buy us too."

Books

Butler, Mary G. *Sojourner Truth: From Slave to Activist for Freedom*. PowerPlus Books, 2003.

Gilbert, Olive. *Narrative of Sojourner Truth*. The 1884 edition, with an introduction and notes by Nell Irvin Painter. Penguin Books, 1998.

Krass, Peter. *Sojourner Truth: Antislavery Activist* (Black Americans of Achievement). Chelsea House, 2004.

Kudlinski, Kathleen. *Sojourner Truth: Voice for Freedom*. Aladdin, 2003.

Roop, Peter, and Connie Roop. *Sojourner Truth* (In Their Own Words). Scholastic, 2002.

Video

Life of Sojourner Truth: Ain't I a Woman (DVD). Phoenix Learning Group, 2008.

Web Sites

mars.jpl.nasa.gov/MPF/rover/about.html
The Mars rover Sojourner was named for Sojourner Truth. Sojourner's 1997 mission is documented on this site maintained by the Jet Propulsion Laboratory of the National Aeronautics and Space Administration.

newpaltz.edu/sojourner_truth/
This site was compiled by Corinne Nyquist, a librarian at the Sojourner Truth Library of the State University of New York at New Paltz. It provides links to photos and other items, mostly connected to the period when Sojourner Truth was known as Isabella, or Belle, and lived in and around Ulster County, New York.

http://tah.collaborative.org/NAEI/
The history of the Northampton Association of Education and Industry is retold in the richly detailed site. Sojourner Truth lived in the 1840s with members of the Northampton Association, which attracted many of the great abolitionists and social reformers of the day.

www.sojournertruth.org/Default.htm
The Sojourner Truth Institute of Battle Creek is located in the Michigan town where Truth spent much of her later life. The Institute's Web site has a detailed timeline of her career, art based on her life and legend, and quizzes and puzzles to test your knowledge about this extraordinary woman.

Index

About the Author

Geoffrey M. Horn has written more than four dozen books for young people and adults, along with hundreds of articles for encyclopedias and other works. He lives in southwestern Virginia, in the foothills of the Blue Ridge Mountains, with his wife, their collie, and five cats. He dedicates this book to his granddaughter Sophia and to his faithful friends at Sojourners' Roost.

Printed in the USA—BG